KEEPING PETS

Cats

Louise and Richard Spilsbury

Heinemann Library
Chicago, Illinois

Customer Service 888-454-2279
Visit our website at www.heinemannraintree.com

Design by Richard Parker and Q2A Solutions
Printed and bound in China by South China Printing Company

10 09 08 07 06
10 9 8 7 6 5 4 3 2 1

Library of Congress Cataloging-in-Publication Data
Spilsbury, Louise.
  Cats / Louise and Richard Spilsbury.
    p. cm. -- (Keeping pets)
  Includes bibliographical references and index.
  ISBN 1-4034-7698-5 (library binding-hardcover)
  1. Cats--Juvenile literature. I. Spilsbury, Richard, 1963- II. Title. III. Series.
  SF445.7S665 2006
  636.8--dc22

                    2005026291

Acknowledgments
The author and publishers are grateful to the following for permission to reproduce copyright
material: Alamy pp. **4t** (Rodger Tamblyn), **10t** (Marc Hill), **29b** (Stefan Solifors); Ardea pp. **5**, **7t**
(Francoise Gohier), **20b**, **23t**, **33** (Dominic Burke), **39t**; Ardea/John Daniels pp. **7b**, **8t**, **8b**, **9b**,
10b, **11**, **13**, **18t**, **19b**, **20t**, **21t**, **25**, **31**, **34t**, **36**, **38**, **39b**, **42**; Corbis p. **41** (James L. Amos);
Dan Nunn p. **45**; FLPA pp. **15t** (Foto Natura Catalogue), **17** (Mark Hamblin); Getty Images
p. **32** (Photonica/Diane Collins); Harcourt Education Ltd/Tudor Photography pp. **14**, **18b**,
23b, **24**, **26**, **27**, **28t**, **28b**, **29t**, **43**, **44**; NHPA pp. **6** (James Warwick), **9t** (Yves Lanceau);
Photolibrary pp. **4b** (Index Stock Imagery/Fotopic), **12** (Survival Anglia/ Marianne Wilding),
30 (Keith Ringland), **34b** (Index Stock Imagery/Pat Canova); Punchstock pp. **1** (Corbis), **19t**
(Corbis); Richard Parker pp. **21b**, **22**, **35**; Ron Kimball p. **15b**; RSPCA pp. **16** (RTL), **37**; SPL p. **40**.

All additional incidental images used courtesy of Getty Images/Photodisc.

Cover photograph reproduced with permission of Ardea/John Daniels.

Every effort has been made to contact copyright holders of any material
reproduced in this book. Any omissions will be rectified in subsequent
printings if notice is given to the publishers.

The paper used to print this book comes from sustainable resources.

Contents

Any words appearing in the text in bold, **like this**, are explained in the Glossary.

What Is a Cat?

Do you know anyone with a pet cat? Chances are that you do, because cats are among the most popular pets in the world.

A type of mammal

Like us, cats are a type of mammal. Mammals are **warm-blooded** animals that have hair on their bodies. Female mammals can feed their young with milk from their bodies. Unlike people, all cats are **carnivores.** This means that they have strong, sharp teeth that they use to kill other animals.

When a cat yawns, he shows off his sharp teeth. All carnivores have teeth like these for eating meat.

Cats can be very friendly pets that make you feel special. But you need to care for them!

Need to know

- It is up to you and your family to take care of your pet. You must give your cat enough food and water. You must help to keep it clean, healthy, and safe.
- It is cruel not to care for pets properly. There are laws in many countries to protect cats and other animals from cruelty.

4

How did cats become pets?

All pet cats are descendants of (related to) African wild cats. In the past, people probably first kept wild cats to protect their food supplies. Cats are very good at hunting mice and other **rodents** that eat stored grain. Over time, some wild cats became domesticated. This means that they became more tame and more comfortable living in people's homes.

In the 18th and 19th centuries, people started to collect unusual-looking cats. Explorers from Europe collected cats from other parts of the world, such as Asia. Soon there were many **breeds** of pet cat, which all looked different.

We know ancient Egyptians had pet cats because of pictures, sculptures, and even mummies of cats found in tombs!

Ancient pet cats

Around 4,000 years ago, ancient Egyptians kept cats as pets because they thought they were very special. They worshipped cats as gods and punished anyone who harmed a cat. However, these are not the oldest pet cats. **Archaeologists** have found bones in ancient graves in Cyprus that are from pet cats that lived 9,500 years ago!

5

Cat Facts

Have you ever noticed that pet cats look a little like tigers or leopards? This is because they are all members of the cat family.

Feline features

There are around 36 **species** in the cat family. Most have a long, strong body with a long tail. Their feet are wide, with soft pads underneath. They can fold their sharp, hook-shaped claws in and out of the tips of their toes. Cats' heads are usually rounded, with triangular or rounded ears, big eyes, and whiskers. Many wild cat species have striped or spotted hair patterns that help them remain hidden as they hunt.

Most cats live in a particular area called a **territory.** Cats scratch and leave special scent marks on trees, posts, and other things in their territory. These signs tell other cats to keep away.

Did you know?

- Cats usually live for around fourteen years, but sometimes they live as long as twenty years!
- Male cats are called **toms.**
- Female cats are called queens.
- Baby cats are called kittens.

Pet cats are related to big cats like this leopard. Both big cats and pet cats spend a lot of time sleeping.

Kittens

Queens can start having kittens when they are about six months old. A group of kittens born at the same time from one queen is called a **litter.** Each litter may contain five or six kittens. When kittens are born, their eyes are closed. Their eyes open after two days. Then, the kittens are ready to explore the world around them.

Kittens **suckle** (feed) for around five weeks before they start to eat solid food.

Fun fact

All kittens are born with blue eyes, which then change color over time!

Cats are very **agile**. They can leap and twist in mid-air to make sure they catch their prey.

Smart hunters

Most members of the cat family are excellent hunters. Wild cats need to be good at hunting to make sure they have enough to eat. However, even well-fed pet cats will hunt birds and **rodents** if they get the chance.

Cats have several special features that help them hunt. They find their **prey** using good eyesight and hearing. Cats can see much better than humans, even when it is almost dark. They move silently toward their prey on padded feet. Then, cats run fast to catch their prey with their claws.

Types of Cat

Pet cats can look very different. Some cats come in single colors such as black, white, orange, blue-gray, or chocolate brown. Others are white with patches of another color. The other main hair pattern is tabby. Tabby cats usually have thin black lines and dots on a brown background.

Tabby cats have a striped coat.

Hair type

Most non-**pedigree** (mixed **breed**) cats can have either long or short hair. Some pedigree breeds, such as Siamese cats, always have short hair. Others, such as Turkish Van cats, always have long, silky hair. The Rex cat has short, curly hair. The Sphynx has almost no hair at all, but its skin often has patches of different colors!

Why are striped cats called tabbies?

There was once a type of striped silk cloth made in a place called Al-Attabiya, in Iraq. People named striped cats tabbies because their hair pattern looked like this cloth!

Calico cats have hair in patches of orange, black, and white. This one is long-haired.

Shape and size differences

Cats can look different in other ways:

- Siamese cats have very long, narrow heads with long, pointed ears and sloping eyes.
- Persian cats have a very flat face with a short nose.
- Maine Coons are very large and shaggy.
- Manx cats have no tail.

Pedigree and non-pedigree cats

There are about 80 different breeds of pedigree (purebred) cat. Cats in a breed always have similar-colored hair and eyes. They always have the same body shape. Owners of pedigree cats usually have written records of the other relatives of their cats.

Non-pedigree cats are a mixture of many different breeds. (There are hundreds of different breeds.) It is uncommon to have any information about the ancestors of non-pedigree cats.

Russian blues are a single-color pedigree breed of cat. They always have thick, short, blue-gray hair and green-blue eyes.

Pedigree Birman cats have long, fluffy white hair with patches of gray or brown. They always have blue eyes.

Are Cats for You?

Cat lovers say cats make the best pets because they are smart, interesting, and very friendly. However, not everybody likes cats as pets. If you are thinking of choosing a cat as a pet, you and your family will need to consider both the good and not-so-good points of having a cat.

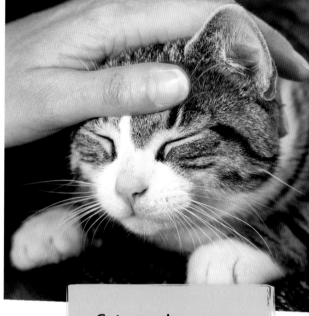

Cats can be very friendly and loving.

Cats can welcome you whenever you come home.

Cat good points

- Cats are intelligent and have great personalities.
- Cats can be very playful and can help you to feel relaxed.
- Cats can be good companions.
- Cats are happy to live in smaller spaces than most dogs.
- Cats are usually very clean.
- Cats live a long time.

Cat not-so-good points

- Cats are very independent and have strong personalities. Some cats are moody and do not like to be handled. Others insist on being near you all the time!
- Cats may scratch and ruin furniture, carpet, and other things in your home.
- Cats are a much longer commitment than pets that live for a shorter time, such as mice or rabbits.
- Cats are expensive to feed and take to a veterinarian.
- Cats may try to kill any **rodents** or birds that you have as pets.

Cats can easily damage things in your home.

Yes or no?

Are you ready to say yes to living with a pet cat? Do you want to share many years of your life with a clean, intelligent animal? If so, then it is time to think about which cat to choose.

11

Choosing Your Cat

When choosing your pet cat, there are several things you will need to consider.

One or more?

Most cats will happily live alone with a family. However, if your family is away from home a lot, it might be good to get two cats so that they can keep each other company. If a cat on its own gets bored, it may start damaging your home!

Of course, two or more cats cost more to feed and care for. They need more space in your home. Like people, cats enjoy their own space from time to time. If you already have an adult cat, watch it carefully if you get a new kitten. Introduce the kitten to the adult gradually, or else they may fight. Make sure you give both animals a lot of attention.

Adult cats should soon get used to a new kitten in their home.

Male or female?

Toms and **queens** both make friendly pets. Whichever sex of cat you choose, you should have them **neutered.** Neutering is a simple, painless operation carried out by a veterinarian. It stops cats from having kittens. Each year millions of kittens are born that cannot be cared for properly. Many end up in **animal shelters.**

Un-neutered cats often try to wander away from home, and they might get into fights. Un-neutered toms may spray smelly **urine** around your home to remind other cats it is their **territory.**

What age?

The age of the cat you choose is important. Kittens are usually more playful than older cats, but they need a lot of attention. You will have to teach kittens to use a **litter box** and not to scratch things.

Adult cats should be **house-trained** and calmer. They may already be used to busy homes. However, some adult cats may not adjust to a new home. Some try to return to their previous home.

Age limit

Remember that kittens should not leave their mothers until they are at least eight weeks old.

Kittens love playing together, especially if they are from the same **litter.**

13

Pedigree or non-pedigree?

Most people have non-**pedigree** (mixed-**breed**) cats. In general, they are less fussy and less likely to get sick than pedigree (purebred) cats. Non-pedigree cats are easier to find because they are always available at **animal shelters**. They also make great family pets.

Some people choose pedigree cats. Different breeds have some typical ways of behaving that may affect whether you choose them as pets. The table on the right shows a few examples. Whichever breed you choose, bear in mind that, just like people, all cats are different. Not all cats behave in the typical way for their breed.

Long-haired cats

You will need to brush long-haired cats every day to keep their hair smooth and tangle-free. Even if you brush them, long-haired cats will still leave hair around your home. It will collect on the floor, curtains, sofas, and clothing. It takes time to clean it up. People with **asthma** or breathing problems should avoid long-haired breeds, because the hairs could affect their health.

Top tip
A long-haired kitten usually grows up to become a long-haired adult.

Long-haired cats cannot help leaving hair around your home.

Know your breed

Breed	Characteristics
Birman	Very calm
Siamese	Can cause a lot of damage in the home
	Has a very loud, wailing meow
	Demands a lot of attention
Persian	Not very active; likes to lounge around
Turkish Van	Enjoys water
	A large, long-haired breed that does not need much **grooming**
Maine Coon	Good with children and dogs; is intelligent and calm
	Likes to scratch things, so needs a scratching post
Korat	Dislikes sudden, loud noises

Most Siamese cats are quite demanding. They will try to get your attention when you are doing other things.

Maine Coon cats can get too big for a small or frail person to lift easily. They also eat quite a lot of food.

Where to get your cat

There are many places to get a pet cat. You could ask friends, neighbors, or your local veterinarian to find out if anyone has a cat who needs a home. Vets will only suggest cats that are healthy and from a good home.

Some people choose cats from **animal shelters** or **rescue organizations.** Workers in animal shelters check the health of each cat. They may also want to know a lot about your family and home before allowing you to have one of their cats. This is because their job is to make sure that their cats will have happier lives than before. You should choose a rescued cat carefully, though. Some rescued cats are nervous because people have treated them badly in the past. It may take time for a rescue cat to trust you.

Cat **breeders** are the people to go to if you want a particular kind of cat. **Pedigree** breeders keep careful records about their cats. Pedigree cats are expensive, so make sure you go to a respected breeder.

Make sure that the pet store or cat breeder keeps its cats in clean cages.

Many people buy cats from pet stores, but pet stores do not always know much about the background of the cats for sale. You should ask questions about the cat's age, health, and parents. If the people in the store do not know much about the cat, you should get your cat somewhere else.

What to look for

The following tips should also help when choosing your cat:

- Always look for a healthy cat. Check that the cat has bright eyes, smooth hair, and a clean bottom.
- Try to see a kitten with the rest of its **litter** and its mother. Then, you can see for yourself how the mother cares for them.
- Kittens should be playful and alert. Lively kittens will watch or even come to check out your finger if you wiggle it nearby. More nervous kittens may be scared by it.

Top Tip

Be careful when choosing a kitten from a pet store. If kittens are taken from their mothers too early or have traveled a long way to the store, they may get sick.

Try to see several litters of kittens before you make your final choice.

What Do I Need?

Before bringing your cat or kitten home, you need to have everything ready for it. You will need bowls for food and water and many other things. You can buy most of these things in pet supply stores.

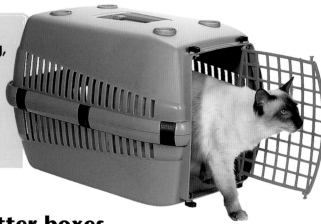

You will need a strong, secure cat carrier to transport your cat home or to a veterinarian.

Litter boxes

Cats need somewhere to go to the bathroom when they are in your home. Most people buy **litter boxes,** which are high-sided plastic boxes. You should fill them halfway with **cat litter.** Cat litter soaks up cat **urine.** Your cat will usually scrape litter over its **feces** (droppings) to cover it up. Most types of litter are made of small pieces of clay, paper, corn, or wood. Cat litter also helps keep the box smelling fresh.

A high-sided litter box stops the cat from kicking too much cat litter onto the floor.

Cat napping

Most cats sleep for about sixteen hours each day! You should make sure your cat has somewhere comfortable, safe, and warm to go that is out of drafts. You can buy a soft fleece bed with a roof, but a basket or cardboard box lined with an old blanket is just as good. Choose bedding that can be washed easily, and remember that whatever you provide, your cat may still choose to sleep on your bed or sofa!

Cats normally sleep for hours each day in their warm, safe bed.

Collar

It is important for your cat to wear a collar, even if it lives indoors all the time. An indoor cat might get out through a window or door that is left open by accident. A cat's collar should have an identity tag with your family name and phone number or address on it. This will help people return your cat to you if it gets lost. The collar should also have a stretchy (elastic) piece in it. This means that if the collar gets caught on something, it will slip off rather than hurt the cat's neck.

Microchipping

Veterinarians can inject a tiny **microchip** under a cat's skin. The microchip holds information that identifies your cat. The best thing about a microchip is that it cannot be removed or accidentally come off a cat if it loses its identity tag or collar.

Identity tags carry information such as your telephone number and the cat's name.

Scratching posts

Cats need to scratch their claws against rough things to keep them in good condition. Some cats may scratch things in your home. To keep them from doing this, provide a scratching post. You can buy many different types or make one out of a tree log that still has its bark on. Cats often like to scratch after waking up, so put the scratching post near their bed.

Cats like big scratching posts because they can climb on them.

Top tips

Does your cat still scratch furniture, even after you gave it a scratching post? Here are two things you can try to stop the scratching:

- Spray a little water at the cat as it is scratching.
- Attach orange peels to the scratched area.

Cats hate water and the smell of orange. Your cat should soon learn to avoid the area!

Toys

Cats love all sorts of toys. You can buy toys or make them from things you can find around your home, such as balls of string, ping-pong balls, or feathers. Make sure the toys are safe. Do not give cats anything they might swallow, such as rubber bands, or things that catch on their claws, such as fine threads. If you do not know which toy to choose, ask other cat owners what their cats prefer.

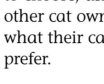

Some cats like to play-fight and bat their toys.

Cats always like to climb inside bags or boxes to find out what is inside.

A variety of toys

Cats, like other animals, need exercise to stay fit and healthy. Without exercise, they may become bored, fat, and unhealthy. You should provide a variety of things for your indoor cat to explore and play with. If it loses interest in one toy, hide it for a while and use another.

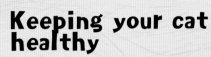

Keeping your cat healthy

- Build or buy a cat condo for climbing and watching the world. Cat condos provide fun and a lot of climbing exercise. They also provide a safe hiding place that is high up. In small apartments, they help provide vertical (up-and-down) space. Place the cat condo near a closed window so your pet can look at life outside.
- Some people buy a full-screen enclosure for their backyard. This allows a cat to exercise outside in safety.
- Hide things for your cat to find. These could be food treats as well as noisy toys inside paper bags or cardboard boxes.
- Cats like to chase things that move fast. Try moving balls of scrunched-up newspaper attached to "fishing poles." Or, try using a mirror to move patches of bright light or blowing soap bubbles to interest your cat.

For a change, some cats enjoy a little safe exercise outside on a leash.

When Your Cat Arrives

Kittens may be more frightened in a new home than adult cats at first, but they usually settle in more quickly.

When you first bring your pet cat home, you will need to gently introduce her to her new world.

A safe house

You need to get a room in your home ready for your new cat:

- Remove any houseplants. Cats can get sick if they chew the leaves of some plants.
- Remove objects that could fall over if the cat jumps on them, such as pots on shelves.
- Keep other pets out of the room for a couple of days. The smell of your other pets will fade, and your new cat will not be frightened by the smell.
- Put down food, water, and a **litter box.**

First steps

Next, bring the cat into the room in a carrier. Close all the windows and doors. Open the cat carrier, but stay nearby. The cat will eventually explore the room. Never frighten the cat by forcing her to come out. When your cat has explored the room, sit by her. Gently talk to and stroke the cat to calm her. Then, introduce her slowly to any other rooms in your home and any other pets.

Litter training

Adult cats will often know how to use a litter box, but kittens need training. Kittens usually need to use the litter box after eating or sleeping. When your kitten wakes up or finishes eating, gently place her in a box of fresh **cat litter**. At first she may not realize what the cat litter is for. Use the litter scoop to show her how to dig in it. Praise the kitten each time she uses the box.

Dealing with a messy cat

If your cat goes to the bathroom away from the litter box, put on a pair of gloves and clean it up. Then, try one of these things to stop the cat from doing it again:

- Move the cat's bed to the soiled area. Cats do not like to make a mess in the place where they sleep.
- Spread aluminum foil on the soiled area. Cats do not like walking or sitting on foil.
- Put a **deterrent** spray on the soiled area. You can get this from a pet supply store or a veterinarian.

There may be a few accidents before kittens learn to use a litter box.

It's okay to say "no" firmly but softly to your cat when she does something wrong. But it is also important to praise her when she does something right.

23

Taking Care of Your Cat

There are some things you must do to care for your pet cat. You must give him food and water each day and you must clean up after him.

Prepared food

Pet cats usually eat cat food bought from pet supply stores, veterinarians, or supermarkets. Cat foods contain meat, some vegetables, and the right balance of **vitamins, calcium,** and other **nutrients** to keep your cat healthy. Food made for other pets, such as dogs, is not good for cats.

You can buy both wet and dry cat foods. Wet food comes in cans or plastic containers. Dry food looks like small pieces of cookie. Different types of wet and dry cat food are suitable for cats of different ages. For example, there is special food for kittens and another for old cats. Cats are often fussy eaters, so it may take a little while before you find out what type of food your cat likes best.

Top tip

Cats like to eat food at room temperature. If you store canned food in the refrigerator to keep it fresh, let the food warm up a little before serving it to your cat.

You should feed your cat in a quiet corner of the kitchen where he will not be disturbed while he eats.

Feeding routine

You should try to feed adult cats at the same time each morning and evening. Kittens need more regular feeding, depending on their age. The following tips should help:

- Put a small amount of food, usually about a third of a cup, in a metal or ceramic (pottery) bowl. These are easier to wash than plastic bowls.
- Place the bowl in the same spot each time.
- Remove any uneaten food from the bowl after mealtimes.

Water

Cats need to drink fresh, clean water every day to remain healthy. They usually drink a lot after feeding, so make sure your cat's bowl is always full. Any bowl you choose should be heavy so that it is not easy to knock over. Some people buy special water fountains for cats to drink from.

A saucer of milk

Milk is a treat for cats. However, it should not be given as a regular drink because it can cause **diarrhea.**

Cats curl their tongues to scoop water up into their mouth.

25

Fresh food

Some people feed their cats freshly cooked meat or fish. Fresh food gives cats some extra **minerals** and ensures they have a balanced diet. Many people feed their cats a little fresh food once or twice a week to make mealtimes more interesting.

Cat treats

Many cats enjoy food treats once in a while. Cat treats from pet supply stores include cookies and **catnip**. Unfortunately, some of these treats contain salt, fat, and chemicals. These things can harm cats if they eat a lot of them. Check to find out what is in the treats you want to buy. Then, you will know exactly what you are giving your pet.

Plants for cats

Many cats like to nibble on grass because it contains minerals. Grass also tickles their throat and makes them **vomit**. Many people think cats do this to clear out their stomach from time to time. Cats also like the smell and taste of catnip or catmint. They like to rub against or roll in this plant.

Cats enjoy freshly cooked meat or fish. However, remember to remove any small bones from meat or fish, because your cat could choke on them.

Cleaning up

It is important to keep your cat's things clean. The **bacteria** that grow on dirty things cause smells and can make cats sick. You should:

- Wash your cat's food and water bowls each week with warm, soapy water. Always wash cat dishes separately from your family's dishes.
- Clean out dirty clumps of **cat litter** from the **litter box** each day using a special scoop.
- Completely empty the litter box into the garbage. Do this once a week with regular litter and less frequently with clumping litter. Wash the box and scoop using a pet **disinfectant** and water. Ask at your pet supply store which disinfectant is best. When the box is clean, dry it and add fresh cat litter. Always wash your hands carefully when you have finished.

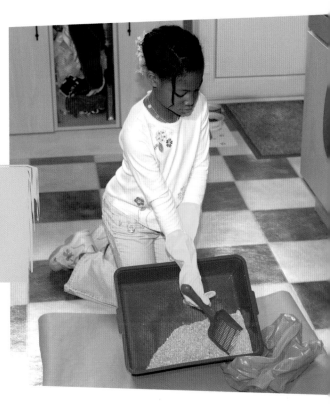

You will need to check the litter box regularly to see if it needs to be cleaned out.

Warning

You should always wear rubber gloves whenever you clean out a dirty cat litter box. Some tiny bugs in cat **feces** can cause serious diseases.

27

Grooming your cat

Cats normally spend a lot of time cleaning their hair and skin. This is called **grooming.** Grooming removes dust, dirt, and loose hairs. Short-haired cats can groom themselves well, but long-haired cats need help. Long hair can get stuck or matted together with dirt. Long-haired cats swallow a lot of hair as they groom, forming clumps of hair called hairballs. Although most cats cough up hairballs, hairballs can sometimes block up their stomachs.

Start grooming by gently combing the hair to remove any tangles. Then, use a soft brush to smooth the combed fur. Be careful around the cat's face.

Grooming

- Most cats love to be groomed. Enjoy this time with your pet.
- You will need a metal comb and a soft bristle brush. Ask your pet supply store or veterinarian which ones are best for your cat.
- Wear some old clothes and brush your cat over an old cloth to catch the loose hair.
- Your cat needs to be calm before you groom her belly, legs, and toes. If she is not calm, she might scratch you. Talk gently to your cat so that she relaxes.

28

Vacations

Your cat needs to be taken care of every day, even when you go on vacation. Some people take their cat with them, but this is not always possible. Most cats like to live in the place they know well. It is best to get someone you know and trust to care for your cat in your home. If this is not possible, you may be able to find a professional **cat sitter** who will be able to do this job for you.

If this is impossible, you can take your cat to stay in a local **kennel**. These have workers whose job is to care for cats. You could ask a veterinarian to recommend a place or you can visit one first to see what it is like. You will have to pay for the cat to stay there. You will also need to have records proving your cat has had regular **vaccinations** (see page 37). You will need a pet carrier to transport the cat.

Cats are happy to stay at home when you are away, as long as someone can come by every day to care for them.

Kennels like this provide a safe temporary home for your cat when you are not around.

29

Flea protection

You may notice fleas or flea droppings when you brush your cat. Fleas are a common problem for cats. They live on cats and feed on their blood. Their tiny bites make your cat's skin itchy. You can buy powders, sprays, drops, and even flea collars at pet supply stores or from a veterinarian to get rid of fleas. Many people use drops that you apply to the cat's back.

To get rid of fleas completely, you will need to treat your house, too. Fleas lay eggs on cats as well as on carpet and other surfaces. Baby fleas hatch and can survive for months before they have the chance to jump onto a passing cat. You should vacuum carpets and curtains and wash cat bedding regularly. You can also use sprays from pet supply stores to treat these places.

Usually the first sign of fleas is when your cat scratches himself a lot.

Where do fleas come from?

Cats can catch fleas from many places, including:

- Other cats and dogs
- Carpets, curtains, and bedding in your house, if they have fleas living in them
- Grass and other plants outside.

Worms

Cats commonly have roundworms and tapeworms living inside them. Cats get worms accidentally by swallowing worm eggs off the ground or when they **groom**. The eggs hatch into adult worms in the cat's **intestines.** Worms do not seriously harm cats but may give them **diarrhea**, make them weak, or make their bottom itchy. Some warning signs that a cat has worms are a swollen belly or when a cat licks its bottom a lot.

You can treat cats for worms by giving them de-worming pills bought from a veterinarian or a pet supply store. You will need to repeat this every few months or your cat will get worms again.

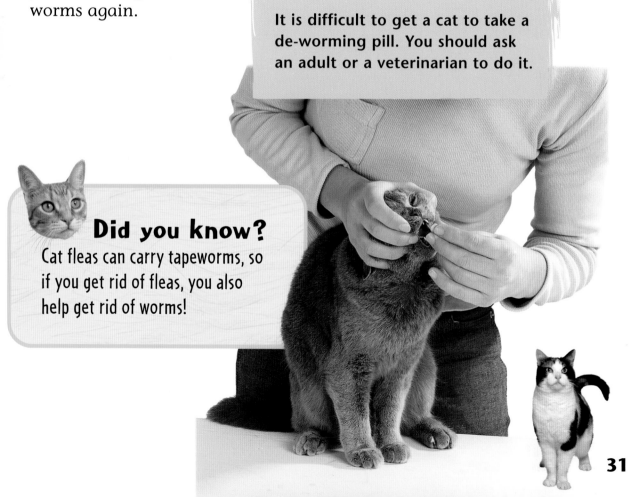

It is difficult to get a cat to take a de-worming pill. You should ask an adult or a veterinarian to do it.

Did you know?
Cat fleas can carry tapeworms, so if you get rid of fleas, you also help get rid of worms!

Living with Your Cat

It takes a little while to get used to living with your pet cat. You need to know how to handle her properly and understand her moods. You also need to know what to do if there are any problems.

Picking up your cat

You need to pick a cat up carefully so that you don't scare or hurt her. Follow these steps:

- Put one hand under your cat's chest, just behind her front legs.
- Place the other hand under the back of her back legs.
- Lift the cat up into your bent arm to support her.
- Don't hold the cat if she struggles to get away when you pick her up. If you hold on, you'll make her unhappy and she may scratch or bite you.
- Do not drop the cat after holding her. Place her gently down on the floor.

Warning
Never pick up a cat by the scruff (back) of its neck. Picking up a cat like this can damage its neck muscles.

You must support a cat properly when you pick it up.

Petting and stroking your cat

It is important to stroke and handle your cat gently. Only do it when your cat is awake. If you touch your cat while she is sleeping, you may frighten her.

Always stroke cats in the direction that their hair grows. Most cats enjoy being stroked in particular places on their body. You could try softly under the chin, around the ears and chest, and around the neck and upper back.

A happy cat purrs loudly and closes its eyes because it is feeling very safe and comfortable.

Togetherness

Cats usually decide when they want to be stroked and cuddled. Many cats enjoy sitting on your lap in the evening. Some may stomp on you before they settle down. Stomping is when cats use their paws to press on your clothes while purring, sometimes with their nose very close to you.

When cats get rough

Some cats can rapidly change mood when they are being stroked. They can change from being calm to being very angry. The cat is telling you to stop! Leave it alone for now. Next time, try stroking its head and neck rather than its back or belly.

33

Knowing your cat's moods

Cats cannot tell you how they feel using words. They show their moods by changing their face and body positions. For example, when a cat is angry or ready to attack, it lowers its head and twists its ears back. Its eyes narrow and it looks straight ahead. However, when a cat is frightened or feels unsafe, it crouches down. It lowers its ears, opens its eyes wide, and often looks away from you.

It takes time for you to understand these different signals. However, be patient and try to learn what your cat wants to tell you.

One way to tell if a cat is angry or playful is if its tail is twitching.

Cat sounds

Cats make about eight different "meow" sounds. They use them to tell you different things, such as when they want food, when they want you to open a door, or even to tell you when they are unhappy. They also make spitting, hissing, and growling sounds, usually when they are frightened or angry.

Even though he can't talk, it is clear that this cat wants to go through the door!

Unusual behavior

Sometimes your cat might do something strange, such as licking plastic bags or panting while crouching low. Cats often do things like this when they are nervous. A cat may feel nervous because something at home is different, such as the arrival of a new pet or a change of routine. Help your cat feel secure by giving her a lot of attention and a quiet, safe place to rest.

Cures for boredom

Sometimes cats get bored. Here are some examples of strange things they do if they get bored:

- Some cats chew cloth or woolen material. Fluff from cloth and clothes can block the stomach of a cat, so keep them out of the cat's way if possible.
- Some cats **groom** themselves so much that they damage their own skin. Try to break the habit by putting a few drops of orange juice on the cat's hair. Cats do not like to lick orange juice.
- Some cats jump out to scratch or paw you when they are bored. If they always leap out at you in the same place, throw a cuddly toy before you pass through so they can attack that instead!

You can cure boredom by playing with your cat and giving her more toys and exercise.

Some cats will attack your legs if they get bored. Don't worry—they usually just want to play!

Cat Health

Cats usually remain healthy if they are fed and cared for properly. An important part of cat care is keeping an eye on your pet's health. You will know your cat very well and will soon spot any changes to his health. If you are unsure about your cat's health, ask an adult to take him to a veterinarian to be examined.

Remember that your pet can get sick quickly, so contact a vet as soon as possible.

A healthy cat will have bright, clean eyes, a pink mouth, and white teeth.

Veterinary checks

It is important to take your cat to a veterinarian each year for a checkup. Veterinarians will check the cat's ears, mouth, hair, and claws for any problems. They will also give yearly **vaccinations**.

Healthy cats

A healthy cat should be active, alert, and happy. It should have smooth, well-**groomed** fur. Its eyes should be clear, clean, and bright. Its ears should be clean and pink inside. Its teeth should be white and its gums should be pink.

Vaccinations

Cats are at risk from several serious diseases. These include cat flu, feline enteritis, feline leukemia, and FIV. Cat flu causes sneezing, sticky eyes, and sometimes breathing problems in cats. The other diseases may kill cats quickly unless they are treated as soon as possible.

Vaccinations keep cats from getting sick in the first place. A veterinarian injects a special fluid called a vaccine under a cat's skin. The **injection** does not hurt your cat. Veterinarians give the first vaccination to a kitten when it is about nine weeks old. After that, the cat will need a booster vaccination each year to keep it safe. You will get a certificate from the veterinarian that proves your cat is vaccinated.

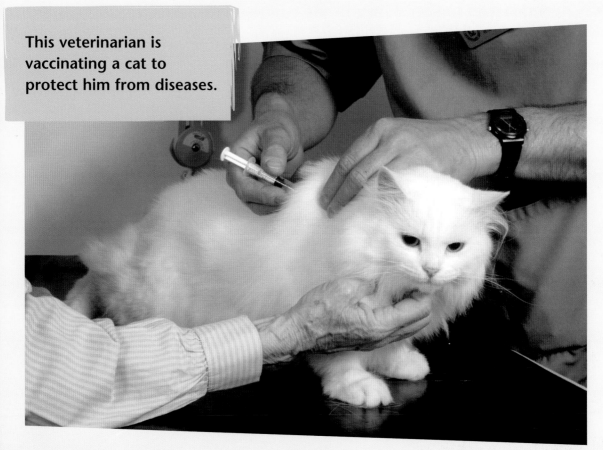

This veterinarian is vaccinating a cat to protect him from diseases.

Sore mouth

Wild cats naturally wipe their teeth clean as they chew **prey**. Pet cats, especially those that eat mostly soft food, cannot clean their teeth so well. **Bacteria** grow on dirty teeth, leaving a yellow coating called plaque. This causes gum disease.

Cats with gum disease have bad breath and have bright red or grayish gums. They find it painful to eat. You can prevent gum disease in your cat by cleaning his teeth with cat toothpaste from a veterinarian or pet supply store. Ask an adult to rub the toothpaste on the teeth carefully using a piece of soft cloth or a pet toothbrush. Some cats do not like having their teeth cleaned. They may bite or scratch until they get used to it. If plaque cannot be brushed off, take your cat to a veterinarian. They will give your cat an **injection** to keep him still. He will not feel anything while the veterinarian scrapes off the plaque.

Top tip

Some adult cats do not like to have their teeth cleaned. Start cleaning your cat's teeth while he is young so he gets used to it. Begin with a few teeth at a time and build up until you can clean the whole mouth.

You can brush your cat's teeth to keep his mouth healthy.

Waxy ears

Cats usually have some wax in their ears. If there is a lot of dark brown, grainy wax, this may mean your cat has ear mites. Ear mites are animals that look like very tiny crabs. Ear mites irritate your cat and make him shake his head or scratch his ears roughly. Scratching can damage the skin of the ear. You can get rid of ear mites using ear drops from a veterinarian.

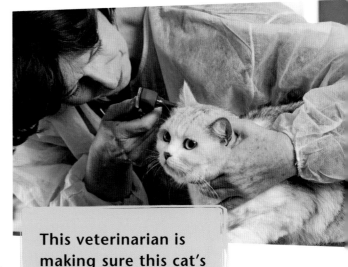

This veterinarian is making sure this cat's ears are healthy, using a special tool to look inside them.

Warning

Never clean the inside of your cat's ears, because you might damage his hearing.

Third eyelid

Cats have a third eyelid called a haw. It protects the eye from drying out. If you can see the haw all the time, then your cat is sick and should be taken to a veterinarian.

Sore eyes

Sometimes a cat's eyes may become red and sticky with thick tears. This is a sign of an eye **infection** caused by scratching or by something rubbing under the cat's eyelid. A veterinarian can give the cat special eye drops to clear up the infection. The veterinarian might say that you should clean the eyes carefully using cotton balls dipped in cooled, boiled water. Ask an adult to help you.

The third eyelid stops a cat's eye from getting too dry.

Wounds

If your cat has a small wound like a bite or scratch, it should heal very quickly. It will take much longer to heal if the wound gets infected. To keep a wound clean, bathe it with salty water. Use one teaspoon of salt in half a pint (250 milliliters) of water.

If your cat has a large cut or wound, you should take him to a veterinarian. You should also take your cat to a vet if the wound is dirty or does not start to heal within a few days. The vet will give you **antibiotic** cream to put on the cat's wound. The vet may shave the cat's hair around the wound. This stops dirt in the hair from infecting the wound.

Stomach problems

Cats have sensitive stomachs. If they eat unusual or infected food, they may suffer from stomach problems. These include **diarrhea**, which is runny **feces**, and **vomiting**. Treat these problems by removing any food and by giving only small amounts of water for 24 hours. If the stomach problems last longer than this, take your cat to a veterinarian.

A veterinarian has put a collar on this cat to stop him from licking a wound on his back. This will let the wound heal properly.

Abscesses

An abscess is an **infection** deep under the skin. This causes a swollen lump, filled with pus, that is painful and makes your cat feel sick. You will need to take your cat to a veterinarian. The veterinarian will drain the abscess and provide antibiotics to clear up the infection.

Claws

If cats scratch enough, they usually keep their claws short. However, sometimes claws can get very long or break. They may hurt or catch in things more easily. Take the cat to a veterinarian who will know how to cut claws properly.

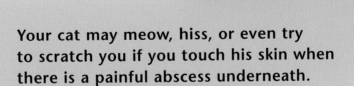

Your cat may meow, hiss, or even try to scratch you if you touch his skin when there is a painful abscess underneath.

Warning

Never try to cut a cat's claws yourself, because you may hurt him or damage his toes.

Growing Old

Most cats live for around twelve to fifteen years, but some cats live for up to twenty years. As they grow old, cats change. Here are some of the changes:

- Their hair may become thinner and some teeth may fall out.
- They become less active.
- They may have a few more accidents around the house, leaving **urine** or **feces** away from the **litter box.**
- They may become grumpier.
- Some older cats may want to be stroked less, but some want more attention than ever before.

Older health

It is important to help an older cat stay healthy. You will need to give your cat food designed for older cats. This food will give it energy even when it does not eat as much as it used to. You will probably need to take the cat to a veterinarian more regularly than before for health checkups. Keep the cat happy by helping out with **grooming,** keeping it company, and by being patient.

Old cats may spend most of their time asleep in a favorite spot.

The right time

Eventually, life may become miserable for a very old cat. It may not be able to recover from illness, clean itself, or eat properly. This might be the time to take the cat to a veterinarian to end its life. The veterinarian will give the cat gas or an **injection** that stops its breathing. Neither the gas nor the injection hurt your cat. It is kinder to end a suffering cat's life like this than to let it live on in pain or misery.

Losing a friend

It is really hard when a pet dies. You will feel very sad because you have lost a friend. Your home may feel empty. Talk about your feelings to your family and friends. Most people will understand how you are feeling. In time, you will remember the good times you had with your pet.

Photographs are a good way to always remember a much-loved pet that has died.

Keeping a Record

Pet cats usually live long and full lives. If you have a good memory, you might be able to remember a lot about your pet. To make sure you do not forget too much, why not keep a record? Then, you can remind yourself about all the happy times you shared with your cat.

Cat scrapbook

You could buy a scrapbook or make one out of construction paper. Collect photos of your cat at different ages and paste them in. How has your cat changed over time? You could include information about your cat, such as when and where you got him, his favorite foods, the different meows he makes, the games he likes to play, and so on.

Diary entries

You could keep a diary section in your scrapbook where you write down what happens at different times during the cat's life, such as:

- What did your cat do when he first arrived at your home?
- When does your cat have his **vaccinations**?
- When does he go to a **kennel**?
- How many hours a day does he sleep or play?

Your scrapbook can be a record of your cat when he was just a tiny kitten!

Find out more

You could find out a lot more information about cats, cat care, cats in history, and record-breaking cats and paste it into your scrapbook. Places to look for information include the Internet and the library. You could also visit cat shows, zoos, wildlife parks, and museums to learn more about different cat **breeds** and other members of the cat family.

Paw prints

We use human fingerprints to identify people, so how about using paw prints in your cat scrapbook? Ask an adult to help you with this activity.

- Cover a table with newspaper or old cloth. Put the open scrapbook on top.
- Make up a bowl of non-toxic, water-based paint.
- Gently dip your cat's paws in the paint.
- Encourage the cat to walk across the scrapbook to leave paw prints.
- Make sure the cat does not lick his paws until you have carefully washed off the paint.
- Allow the paint to dry before closing the book.

Remember to take a lot of photos of your cat, so that you can add them to your scrapbook.

45

Glossary

agile   able to move quickly and easily

animal shelter   place where abandoned or badly treated pets are cared for

antibiotic   medicine that can cure some animal diseases

archaeologist   someone who studies history by digging up ancient remains

asthma   condition that causes people to have breathing problems

bacteria   tiny living things. Some bacteria are useful, such as those found in yogurt. Other bacteria can cause disease.

breed   kind of cat

breeder   someone who raises a particular kind of animal

calcium   substance used by the body to build strong teeth and bones

carnivore   animal that eats other animals or meat from other animals

cat litter   material put in litter boxes that soaks up urine

cat sitter   someone who visits people's homes to care for their cats while they are away

catnip   plant containing an oil that cats are strongly attracted to

deterrent   something that stops a person or animal from doing something

diarrhea   runny feces (droppings)

disinfectant   spray or liquid that destroys germs

feces   droppings

groom   to clean an animal's fur. Many animals groom themselves.

house-trained   animal that is trained to go to the bathroom outside or in a litter box, not in the house

infection   sickness that makes part of the body fill with pus

injection   when a needle is used to put medicine into an animal's body

intestines   part of the body that leads from the stomach to the anus

kennel   place that cares for people's cats while they are on vacation

litter   number of baby animals born together

litter box   box where cats can go to the bathroom

microchip   tiny piece of material used to store a lot of information

minerals   different substances used by the body for various purposes

neutered   when part of an animal's sexual organs are removed so that it cannot reproduce (have babies)

nutrient   part of food that an animal's body needs to grow and keep healthy

pedigree   when a purebred animal has a list of its ancestors

prey   animal that gets eaten by other animals

queen   female cat

rescue organizations   groups that care for abandoned pets

rodent   animal, such as a mouse, with strong front teeth that keep growing throughout its life

species   kind or type of animal

suckle   when a baby mammal drinks milk from its mother's body

territory   patch of land that an animal thinks of as its own

tom   male cat

urine   liquid waste from the body

vaccination   getting an injection that protects an animal against a disease

vitamin   nutrient found in food. Animals need certain vitamins to keep them healthy.

vomit   to throw up

warm-blooded   describes an animal that can warm up or cool down to adapt to its surroundings

Further Reading

Crisp, Marty. *Everything Cat: What Kids Really Want to Know About Cats.*
    Chanhassen, Minn.: NorthWord, 2003.

Dennis-Bryan, Kim. *Kitten Care*. New York: DK, 2004.

Jeffrey, Laura S. *Cats: How to Choose and Care for a Cat*. Berkeley
    Heights, N.J.: Enslow, 2004.

Waters, Jo. *The Wild Side of Pet Cats*. Chicago: Raintree, 2005.

Useful Addresses

The following organizations work to protect animals from cruelty.
They also help people learn how to care for their pets.

**The American Society for
the Prevention of Cruelty
to Animals (ASPCA)**
424 E. 92nd Street
New York, NY 10128
Tel: (212) 876-7700

**The Humane Society of the
United States (HSUS)**
2100 L Street NW
Washington, D.C. 20037
Tel: (202) 452-1100

Internet
There are hundreds of pet websites on the Internet. The following
sites give information about caring for animals, including cats.

http://www.aspca.org
The website of the American Society for the Prevention of Cruelty to
Animals (ASPCA). Under "Pet Care," check out "Cat Care."

http://www.hsus.org
The website of the Humane Society of the United States (HSUS).

You can also use the Internet to find out about cat clubs in your
local area.

Disclaimer
All the Internet addresses (URLs) given in this book were valid at the time
of going to press. However, due to the dynamic nature of the Internet, some
addresses may have changed, or sites may have changed or ceased to exist since
publication. While the author and publishers regret any inconvenience this may
cause readers, no responsibility for any such changes can be accepted by either
the author or the publishers.

Index